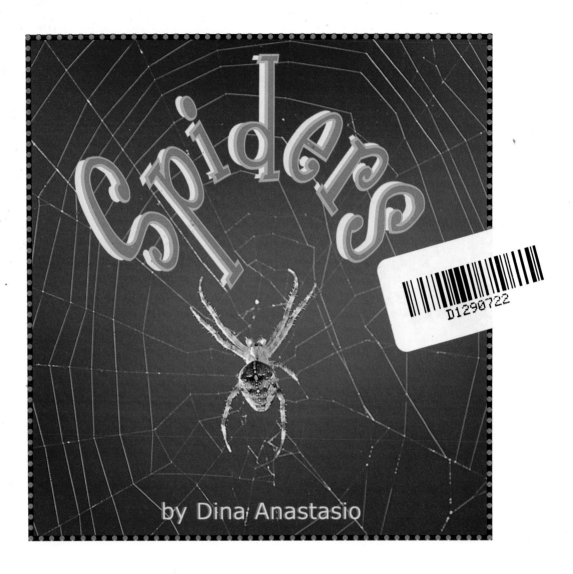

Spiders

by Dina Anastasio

SCHOLASTIC INC.
New York   Toronto   London   Auckland   Sydney
Mexico City   New Delhi   Hong Kong   Buenos Aires

Developed by Kirchoff/Wohlberg, Inc., in cooperation with Scholastic Inc.
Credits appear on the inside back cover, which constitutes an extension of this copyright page.
ISBN 0-439-35100-6
7 8 9 10   23   09 08

What is a spider? You may have seen one hiding in a corner. Or you may have seen one in a web.

Spiders are very special animals. Many people think spiders are insects. Spiders are not insects. Spiders belong to a group of animals called arachnids.

There are many kinds of spiders. Some are tiny. Some are big. They may be yellow, blue, purple, or black.

Spiders move around quietly on eight legs. They see with four pairs of eyes. Their work makes them special.

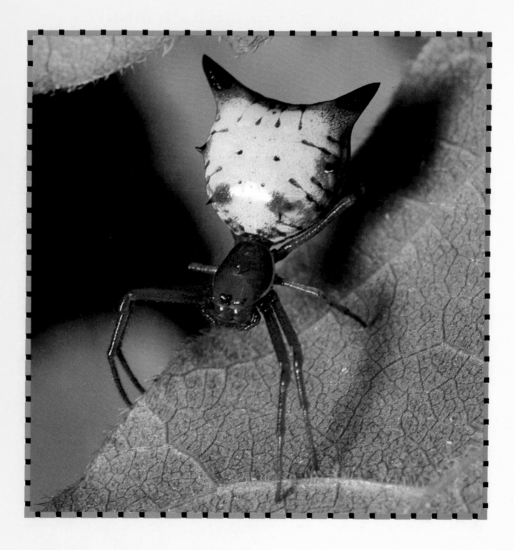

All spiders spin silk. Their bodies make sticky silk threads. Spiders use them to build things. They spin parachutes to ride the wind. They spin safety nets to catch themselves.

Some spiders spin webs. They stick the ends of their silk threads to a surface such as a rock or a wall. The threads become very strong. The spiders can walk on them. Their webs can be very beautiful.

How do spiders know how to spin webs? No one teaches them. They just seem to know. This is called instinct.

Most spiders need webs. Spiders eat flies and ants. They eat other insects too. They catch insects in their webs.

Some spiders do not spin
webs to catch their food. These spiders
hunt for food. They use their fangs to get food.
Jumping spiders hide. When they see
something tasty, they jump. Then they have
something to feast on. Most hunting spiders see
very well. They have better eyesight than
spiders that spin webs.

Spiders use their silk in other ways too. Many spiders spin cocoons. The silk cocoons keep the spiders' eggs safe.

The mother spiders hang the cocoons. Soon the eggs hatch. Most baby spiders care for themselves.

Spiders spend most of their time alone. They do not seem to need company. Even baby spiders spend time alone. They leave after they hatch. The baby spiders can spin their own webs.

Spiders live everywhere.
They live in the woods. They live in
caves. They live in barns and houses.
Fishing spiders are found at ponds. They
are hunters. They run across ponds looking for
food. To a fishing spider a pond looks like a
smooth tray on which to run.

Crab spiders are tiny. Their bodies are flat. Most crab spiders move like crabs. They move forward. They move backward. They move from side to side. Crab spiders hunt for their food. They grab food with their fangs.

Most spider babies take care of themselves. African wolf spiders are different. African wolf spiders carry their babies on their backs.

African wolf spiders are hunters. They live under the ground. There they wait for an insect to come by.

Trap-door spiders live under the ground, too. They spin silk. They use the silk to line their homes. They use silk and earth to build trap doors. The doors fit just right. They snap shut. They even have silk hinges!

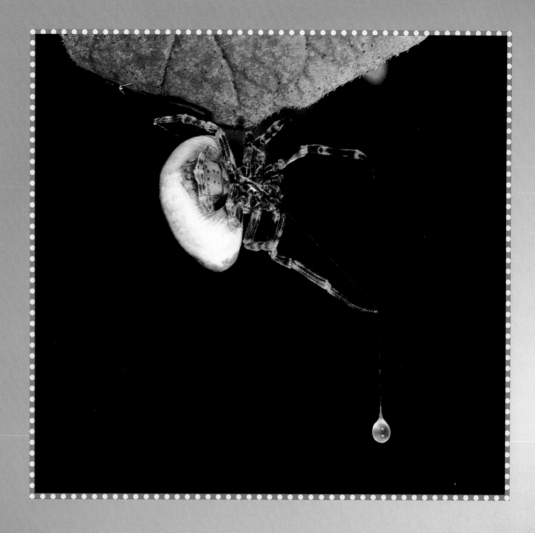

A bolas spider spins one thread. The thread has a sticky end. The sticky end catches food.

Bolas spiders use their threads to go far and high. They just hang on and swing.

The tarantula is a big hairy spider. It looks more dangerous than it is. It cannot see well. It hunts at night.

Some spiders are poisonous. The bite of a black widow spider can make a person sick. Black widows bite when they are in danger.

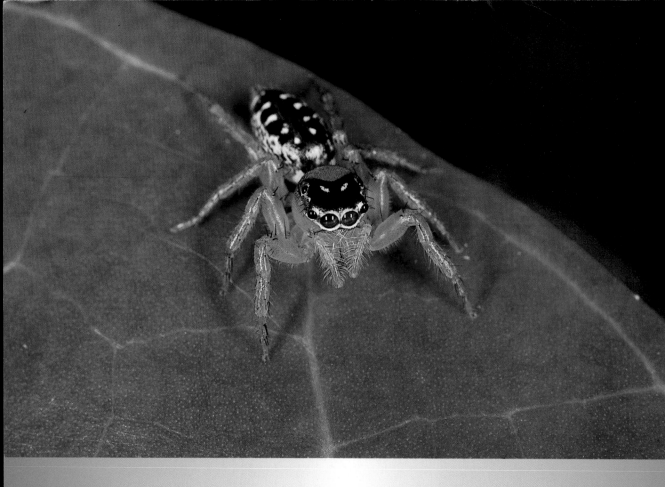

Facts About Spiders

1. All spiders have eight legs.
2. Most spiders have four pairs of eyes.
3. Spiders have fangs.
4. All spiders have a body with two parts.
5. All spiders spin silk. Some kinds of spiders spin webs.